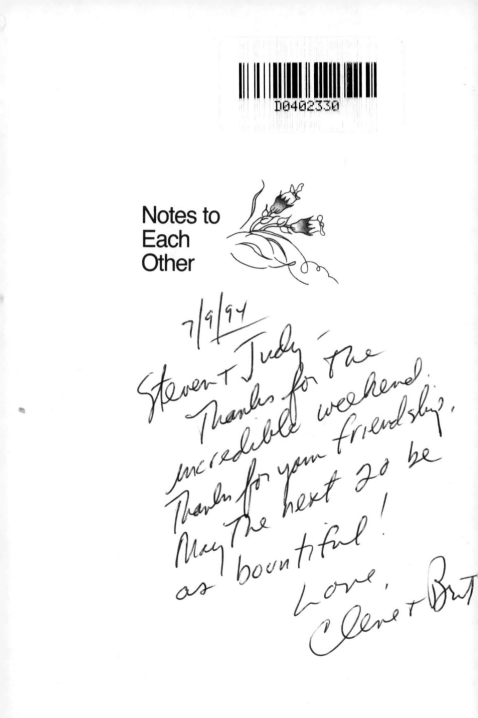

Notes to Each Other

7/9/94

Steven + Judy –
Thanks for the
incredible weekend.
Thanks for your friendship.
May the next 20 be
as bountiful!
Love,
Clene + Brit

Notes to
Each
Other

Hugh and Gayle Prather

Bantam Books
New York   London   Toronto   Sydney   Auckland

NOTES TO EACH OTHER
A Bantam Book
Bantam hardcover edition / May 1990
Bantam trade paperback edition / May 1991

Designed by M 'N O Production Services, Inc.

Illustrations by Claudia Stevens.

ISBN 0-553-35282-2

Published simultaneously in the United States and Canada

*Bantam Books are published by Bantam Books, a division of Bantam
Doubleday Dell Publishing Group, Inc. Its trademark, consisting of the
words "Bantam Books" and the portrayal of a rooster, is Registered in
U.S. Patent and Trademark Office and in other countries. Marca
Registrada. Bantam Books, 666 Fifth Avenue, New York, New York
10103.*

PRINTED IN THE UNITED STATES OF AMERICA

FFG   0 9 8 7 6 5 4 3 2 1

For Jerry and Diane

How This Book Was Compiled

Like *Notes to Myself,* this book came mostly from a stack of yellow sheets where we jot down our ideas and insights. Usually this is done just as we are going to bed. We will be talking and one of us will say, "That should be written down." The person recording it often adds other ideas and so the result is a mixture. The final manuscript was written very much the same way—a trading back and forth, each of us adding and editing. Even though the book at times takes the form of a dialogue, it would have been misleading for us to have designated each note as Hugh's or Gayle's, because not only have we both contributed to every note, we do not have separate positions on what should have been included. As much as is probably possible, this book is written with one voice, and although it definitely has a progression, it is meant to be dipped into at random.

INTRODUCTION

This diary begins with the commitment we made to each other in 1965 to remain together for life. We were soon to discover that this act alone, although fundamental to creating a climate of trust in which love can grow, does not solve all problems, and we want you to understand that we did not begin as a well-matched couple or with any other advantage except this commitment. We were not brought together through signs and wonders; we did not even particularly love each other. We married on impulse the night of our third date without "hearing a Voice," and things went rapidly downhill from there.

There are very few mistakes that are humanly possible for a couple to make that we have not made, and yet, twenty-five years later, we are each other's best friend and greatest pleasure. We are in truth each other's purpose and way. As perhaps you will see in this diary, we did not arrive at this outcome through uncommon ability. We simply worked and started over day after day, learning it all from scratch, until gradually we got beyond the struggle. The fact that it is possible for *any* couple to get beyond the struggle is the promise we hope this book will carry.

Perhaps the material that was the most difficult for us to include was our anguish over infidelity during the first thirteen years of our marriage. Gayle grew up in a home that had its share of problems, but a lack of loyalty was not among them, whereas on both sides of Hugh's family infidelity and divorce were a deep and long-standing pattern. Hugh's father was married four times, his mother three, and as a boy his father frequently instructed him by word and example on the "proper" way to carry on an affair. That a real man had them was never questioned.

The year we were married (1965) was the beginning of an unfortunate string of antimonogamous movements in this country ("wife-swapping," "free love," "swinging," "open marriage," etc.) that continue to this day. It was not only Hugh's boyhood indoctrination but the ideals of many of the couples who were close friends that Gayle had to outendure and that Hugh had to see through and overcome. We have included our personal struggles in this area as an aid to those who are going through similar difficulties because we have seen so many couples throw their hands up over less protracted incidences of betrayal than ours, and we know from our own and from our counseling experience that no relationship need be irreparably damaged by these occurrences. *Any* form of pressure on a relationship—infidelity, the death of a child, a business failure, children from another marriage—can be walked beyond. This is always a possibility.

There is something about being known by another person for a very long time that is hard to convey to people who are about to split up. They don't understand the gift they give themselves by refusing to lose faith in another human being. And surely they haven't tasted the deep self-acceptance that can come from knowing that time and again someone has seen them at their worst and still loves them. Duration alone does not bring this miracle, but unremitting devotion does. Certainly there are good reasons for divorce, and we would never advise a couple not to take this step, but how casually it is done! Mindlessly people cast aside a friendship of half a lifetime, destroy their children's one safe harbor, and deny the weeping world's need for a model of real love. And for what? For some shallow self-assertion? for some hollow escape? for some romantic play? And having abandoned their friend, they are left with no one who can see it all, and accept it all. Perhaps now there is someone who offers a teetering excitement, but no one with whom they are deeply comfortable. And no one that they themselves understand so well how to care for, how to make happy, how to heal.

It is this very lack of care that is the great disease of our time. If we look with the same honesty at the society of humans that we give to the study of other species, we cannot fail to see an insensitive and deeply selfish life form. Although the world itself is in our hands, we have not cared for its living creatures, we have not cared for its resources and riches, we have not cared for each other, and we have not cared for ourselves. We litter our own streets. We poison our own air. We dump almost anything into the water we must drink. The wealth of our nations is squandered on things with which to kill each other. We disregard the health of the people for whom we produce our food and torture the animals we raise to eat. We demonstrate appallingly little care for the starving and the disadvantaged, for the elderly and the sick. And so entrenched are we in our self-centeredness that even to mention the obvious stirs up great defensiveness and anger. We do not care, and we do not want to look at our lack of it.

The spawning ground of human selfishness is the insensitivity with which we treat ourselves, our mate, and our children. If the prevailing mood within the home were the same between heads of state, there would be continuous world war. We will even treat a stranger with more courtesy than we treat the members of our own family. Surely there is nothing more important than halting this insanity, for we are breaking a fundamental principle of Nature by living without love, and the survival of the decency and humanity of the human race is deeply threatened by our present course.

So many now behave as if their partner existed on a lower level than friends or pets or other forms of life. They can feel quite strongly about the plight of coal miners or the treatment of laboratory animals, and yet somehow the feelings of their own spouse do not matter in any deep sense. They believe that all they have to do is say the magic words, "It's different between us now. Something is missing," and they can turn their backs on this lesser human and walk away. The fact that another person will not only be made unhappy, but dealt a blow that may never heal, is just part of the stuff songs are made of, the game of love the rules of which anyone should know, and certainly no reason to consider not acting out their latest infatuation or newly conceived chance at personal advancement.

How can it hinder happiness or true attainment to make simple commitment a part of one's soul and being? How can it hurt someone to take a friend for life and to let that be that? And how can we heal the world of people we have not seen if we cannot love and treat fairly the people we see?

Notes to
Each
Other

Few people believe they have the right body, and yet they do not destroy it. Many think they did not get the children they deserve, and yet they would never desert them. Most people will not even abandon a dog. Why then is it so impossible to say, "You are my friend. I will never leave you"?

It is not. And I say this to you now:
You are my partner, the one I want to walk through life with, the one I want to grow old with, the one whose hand I want to hold as I die. I will never neglect you. I will never turn from you. Forever and forever, I will never leave you.

I promise not to question your needs
I promise not to examine your actions
I promise not to second-guess you
or anticipate you
or in any other way to contrast
myself with you
I will receive and hold
you still in my mind
newly born this instant
a child of now
worthy of an attention so broad
and complete and void of calculation
that it can only be called love

Relationships have become the new focus. It is very chic now to plot and graph them during lunch break. Most people view their marriage or new relationship as a thing wholly separate from their real life. It's talked about like a new Jacuzzi whose performance can be rated and that one is free to get in and out of at will. Thus the partner is not a real person but a function. And it's obviously not a part of this function to be inconvenient.

But people are people. They are not career support, or sexual experiences, or an escort service on our daily rounds. They are not the destroyer of our enemies, or a way of killing time. They are not even a means to get us to the next level. They are not here to give to us or to withhold. They *are* us.

Friendship means no separate heart.

Today we want our partner to be like a doll that has no needs of its own, that can be picked up when it's wanted, that has a certain look and can do certain things with its mouth and body, that remains the same age and retains the same set of attitudes within its features. And for this we will give it love—until we have outgrown it and, for the sake of our growth, must cast it aside.

Be the dawn of my day
The wings of my morning
Be my beacon and my star
But, please, don't be demanding

In the course of every long-term relationship, one's partner will change, and this need not come as a devastating blow. From the time they are born to the time they leave home, children undergo enormous change and dramatic periods of adjustment. They try out new behavior and make numerous mistakes. Yet their place in their parent's heart is secure, for no matter what transformations they undergo, in the eyes of a loving mother or father, they are always cherished.

It is generally understood that all of this is quite normal, and yet most of us seem ill prepared for the fact that adults undergo just as many changes as children. Although we believe we are capable of giving our children greater love than our parents gave us, somehow we don't think it's appropriate to respond to personality changes in our mate with the same understanding and patience we would give a child.

Perhaps the primary way we subvert our happiness is to carry with us the question of whether there is something better than whatever is at hand. Maybe there is a better mate, a better child, a better house, a better dog. Thus we prevent ourselves from having the experience of devotion, out of fear that we might blind ourselves to a good change.

The mistake we make is to confuse devotion with liking. We believe that to like *absolutely* is to be devoted. But what have we ever liked absolutely? So we are "justified" in being devoted to nothing. We are not devoted to our children acting their age, to having the physical appearance or intelligence they have inherited, or to trying out certain styles of speech and dress. We are not committed to our mate's mistakes, limitations, and current level of progress. We find endless fault with our dwelling, our neighborhood, and our job.

We think that devotion is to the *object* and that the object must be superior to *deserve* devotion. But devotion is not being on one's knees wiping up the footprints of a saint.

We think that devotion is a behavior, that it's not real unless it looks a certain way. We must spend every waking hour entertaining our children (and parents who put theirs in daycare are therefore guilty). Our house must be kept respectfully clean and orderly (and we must get very upset if anything is out of place or gets broken). Our spouse must not spend long hours on the phone with friends (otherwise he or she is not devoted to us).

But devotion is an act of the heart.

Devotion is the decision to look upon whoever is before me, or whatever is within my hands, with perfect thoughtfulness.

Here's our friend Marjorie who had four kids with a husband she describes as "a very gentle and good person" but who did not attend the meetings, did not meditate, did not use the new language, and so off she went in search of her soul mate and has been dragging her children from city to city for nine years, being uncommitted to everything she tries, and shattering life after life in search of the one, true, unconditional love she has never thought to give.

I can't free myself from a mistake until I acknowledge that I made one.

Attack is the problem, not the answer. A mistake calls not for self-blame, but only for correction.

This afternoon Michael told us that he felt very high after he made the decision to leave Sarah. The signs had been pointing that way for years, and when he met Becky he knew he was right. After all, he had never felt so alive, so attuned with nature and with his deeper self. "Love is the answer all right," he said. "Sarah is having a hard time right now, but I know it all has to work out for her too." And indeed he did seem happy, but it was difficult for us to share his mood. Only the day before we had seen his little girl in the school office sobbing because she wanted to spend Christmas with both her parents.

The difference between euphoria and peace is kindness.

If you're going to leave me for your new love, please just leave me. Don't try to convince me it's divine guidance. God does not have pets.

There we are in bed, you flat on your back, pillows under your knees, an orthopedically aligned person who forgot to lock the front door and turn off the lights. We look at each other, guilt already assigned, and the question of who will get up lying between us like a dirty look. But I see in your eyes that ancient fear that I will mistake forgetfulness and a bad back for a careless disregard of my feelings. Sometimes it's so easy to love you.

Did I pick the right person? This question inverts the starting and ending points. We do not pick our perfect match because we ourselves are not perfect. The universe hands us a flawless diamond—in the rough. Only if we are willing to polish off every part of *ourselves* that cannot join do we end up with a soul mate.

Relax into your destiny.

Acceptance does not preclude change, it precludes remaining in conflict.

"Remain in the present" is just another way of saying, "I commit myself to my life."

My life includes all those who are in my life.

Give to this other from the very best part of your mind. Give only with thine eyes. Give, not to change the other—because who can know what change is needed?—but give without sin, that is, give for the sake of giving. It is in the pure act of giving that you will come to know what you are, where you are, and who is with you.

Giving comes *before* faith and trust. It lends the experience on which they are based.

Giving has great reward but no predictable results.

It's not phony for us to *act* kindly toward each other even when we are *feeling* anxious, depressed, irritated, superior, or any of the other superficial emotions. Just as in meditation, the body can be used in *any* situation as an aid to shifting vision to a deeper level.

Certainly the body can be made to act out a feeling. However, never is only one emotion felt, and although negative emotions are the most noticeable, they are by no means the most central to our core. At any given moment the mind is singling out and making real one feeling over another, for example, a desire for revenge over a desire to forgive. During a moment of estrangement, if we wish consciously to enter into this process of inner selection, our choice will be strengthened if we see to it that our behavior does not undermine it.

How to argue should not be discussed during an argument.

The body is merely a communication device. It's like a telephone that makes and receives calls. If during an argument the body is also getting dressed, or driving, or eating, or any other activity that does not *look* like communication, the two people will have trouble concentrating on each other's point of view, just as they would trying to make themselves heard over a busy signal on the phone. If communication is going to help a relationship rather than destroy it, these little discussions that are carried on while the couple is doing something else must be treated with as much respect as the relationship they threaten.

The usual pattern of our arguments seems to have a life of its own and simply takes us over once we get too deeply immersed in an issue. I can try to break the dynamic by saying nothing, or by running out of the house, or by overreacting and attacking quickly, or by moaning and rolling on the floor as I did last week, but it still ends in the same dissatisfying way. At most I can temporarily frighten you into believing that I am dangerously insane, but this only confirms what you always suspected.

Only love can break hate, it's just that it is so very difficult to feel love at times like these. What we must do is catch the pattern before it possesses us, or at least have an agreed-upon means of halting the conflict long enough to search our hearts for another set of feelings.

Whenever you and I take the time to remember how much we love each other—even if this means playing that silly game of taking turns saying ten good things about the other—a very interesting change in perception occurs. We begin thinking of capitulation as gain. The distance between two positions is bridged through concession. These can be seen either as personal sacrifices or as gifts that strengthen the bond between us.

Love reverses the usual way of arguing, in which people first remember their grievances and then try to come up with the least costly means of personal triumph.

"What should I say? What should I do?" When I am centered on these questions I am attempting to change the form of my relating without changing its content. Behavior *follows* attitude. I want to aim for consistent attitude, not consistent behavior. There can never really be a question of what to do, of *how* to treat each other, because the starting point is a loving state of mind.

Once the mind releases itself into love, there are suddenly a thousand obvious ways to show it.

You already know enough.

What am I *not* doing now that I know to do?

The external picture is an effect. I must therefore work on the cause—my mind—and not get caught up in trying to change the picture. Preoccupation with how the relationship *appears* to be going forces me to believe that the picture is a cause and my mind its effect, thus stripping me of all control and placing me in the role of victim. It does not follow, however, that I can look at the picture, appraise it, and thereby pass judgment on my inner efforts.

A verbal attack is always a call for help. This insight is a switch in perception that repositions me to respond from another level. A verbal attack is clear evidence that the person before me is unhappy. It's like the growl of a hurt animal. There may be nothing outward I can do, and in fact any gesture on my part is likely to be misunderstood, but a counterattack is unnecessary because it's based on a deep misreading of the human condition. All I need see is that to be in pain is innocent. Although this may have no apparent effect on the person's behavior, there are very few people unaware of the difference between being seen as innocent and being seen as guilty.

I thought you would never lie to me. I thought we had agreed that no matter what we had done, or were about to do, we would be completely open. Now I feel as if I am living with a stranger. You certainly have proven you are not my friend. A friend would not deceive and set me up the way you have. You say, "All I wanted was to be free to have a little fun. It was not meant as an attack." Now I find out you have been "having a little fun" for years—and with individuals we both know. Of course it was an attack. You raised a blade above my heart and didn't really care whether it dropped. You would not take chances with your knee or even your car, and yet our love means so little to you that you risk it all just for "a little fun."

Irrational as it may seem to you, I am very angry about the scene you are making—calling your parents, going to our friends. Isn't this equally a betrayal? Look at how many have turned against each other who could have tried a little harder. This useless wreckage of marriages and families is now strewn across several decades. Let's not become part of the litter. We can weather this.

Take my hand, and no matter how long, we will walk out of the night together.

It's true that we got married at a time when open marriage was an exciting new ideal and that I allowed you to pursue it with only mild objection—but don't you see the difference? That was something we both agreed on, something we worked out together in detail, whereas this you have been doing behind my back. That was an experiment of the times that we both can see had devastating results for every couple we knew. Now we are about to have our first child and this little life must come into a place of safety and stability, not a room in hell. Its happiness and mental health are a sacred trust. It will have no other place to turn. It needs to grow up seeing an example of love's possibilities, not learning the sad, tired lessons of how to withdraw, fight, cheat, and break up. The love that this child can give you far exceeds some temporary yearning from an acquaintance. How deeply you could delight yourself, and how happy you could make me, by being a whole parent.

It always seemed that there must be a way to bring a sense of normalcy to my affairs. It was as if the whole world swirled righteously and angrily around an innocent encounter, and if people would just stop being so emotional about two individuals liking each other, everything would be okay. This is one of the reasons I lied to you, so as not to stir things up. I believed that if I only had a more liberated partner I could enjoy myself in peace. But the simple fact is I don't have someone else, I have you. And even if you were more liberated, that would bring its own set of problems—which I don't think I would like any better.

Hidden thoughts can still be felt, sometimes even more acutely. When we went to Albuquerque last year for our anniversary, I kept asking you what was wrong until finally you got angry and I shut up. What was wrong was that you were with me out of duty, not out of love. An affair by its very nature is a dynamic involving more than two people, and the relationship between the various sides is in deep conflict, whether or not all the circumstances are known. To choose an affair is to choose the entire dynamic and peace is not a possibility. You thought that your unhappiness was caused by me, and it's true that there have been times during this I have badly overreacted, but that comes with the affair. If what the two of you were doing was insensitive, how could its effects be any less cruel?

I am truly and deeply sorry. If you will forgive me, I will take my mistake and transform it into a priceless gift, which I will give to you a thousand times a day, until once again you know that I am your friend.

You are enough reason for me to practice forgiveness for a lifetime.

When I realized how programmed you were to be
unfaithful, how deeply ingrained was your mistrust of
a woman's love, how only by ingesting the sad lessons
of your family history could you feel a little safety
within your "privileged" childhood, there was never a
question in my mind that you deserved another chance
and that you could indeed be trusted with my
devotion.

If my devotion allows you to heal the wounds of your
past, can it truly hurt me?

Trust is a present decision that need not consult
the past.

Don't honor your ego even with your guilt.

As we have been having these daily sessions, I have come to see that many relationships were adversely affected besides ours. I don't know how I could have been so blind to this before. There is an ugly trail of broken friendships and broken lives stretching behind me, as it is behind my dad, my uncle, and so many others. I have added very little to the world except a kind of excited misery. I was a poisoner, but now I wish to be one no longer. It has taken me more than these thirteen years of our marriage—because as you know, this behavior began many years before that—but finally I see that there is no sacrifice in giving it up, and I am willing to do whatever it takes to accomplish this—changing occupations, moving, going to a counselor, anything.

I think I somehow believed that I could have both a loving, dedicated relationship with you and an exciting relationship with others. And for a time I thought it was working. But now I see that deception cannot be confined. It's not possible to deceive you and not them, or myself. I was never loved by any of my partners the way I thought I was—because I was not there to be loved. Who can love a half truth? And I couldn't love myself because I was practicing having no self. I can see this sad pattern going back several generations on both sides of my family. I want it to die out with me. Perhaps I will never truly help people, but at least I can stop hurting them.

Now that I am ready to commit, now that I want this relationship more than anything else, you are having second thoughts. You are wondering if you made a mistake. You are wondering if there is someone better. And this has been going on for several months. Although we haven't separated, we are uncommitted. People take questions like these to their graves and miss living their lives. How much longer are we going to be ruled by a question for which we have provided no answer? How can we know to stop giving if we never truly gave? How can we decide to separate if we have never joined?

If you will give me a little time, a little space,
I promise not to use it to love you less.

To love you deeply and well is not to agree with you on all occasions or to say yes to every last whim or to ignore my own needs, even the selfish ones.

It is to be the keeper of your goodness, the one who never forgets who you are and where you are going.

It is not an appearance, an anxious effect, a set of silly courtesies, or some romantic posturing.

It is to choose the vision of my soul, which can never fail to see your deepest longings.

It is the great and final decision that you are as innocent now as the hour you were born.

Why should our love continue to be crippled by all our worn-out dislikes? Let us grow to like. If we can crawl around on the floor together shaking our heads and gooing at the baby, we can do anything. We never say it's against our basic nature to change a diaper. If I have learned to like carrot juice and sprouts and going nowhere on a stationary bike; if I have learned to dislike fatty foods and alcohol and overeating; I can certainly learn to like country music and shopping the malls. I can enjoy always losing at cards and turning my socks right-side-out every time. I can peacefully abide foreplay.

Although they have three boys, the people next door evidently do not believe in childhood. Whenever John plays any game at all in the backyard, or even yells inside the house, we can expect a call. Ever since moving in we have been dreading hearing the phone ring. Their house, however, is better designed for children than ours, and two weeks ago we asked Arnoldo if he would discreetly inquire whether they would be interested in selling. Since hearing that they are considering his offer, we have been looking forward to the same calls that before we feared, knowing that they may indicate a growing dissatisfaction. The phone is the same, the complaints are the same, everything is the same except our interpretation. Applying this same principle to your eating with your mouth open, I have been reminding myself of two facts: I find the way the puppy eats funny and she makes more noise than you. And throughout your childhood the dinner table was a battleground over how you ate. So now when my ego calls me up on the judgment line, I smack a little and answer, "In this house can be heard the sounds of happy eating."

Instead of being preoccupied with what you or I are not getting, with what we no longer have, with what others appear to have that we do not, and countless other lines of deprivation and loss, let us be preoccupied with what is *here,* with what is human, with what is real. Let us look at the negative, but look at it in order to walk beyond it, not to be transfixed by it. Let us be guardians, not just parents. Let our family break bread, not just eat. Let us have a livelihood, not just careers. I want your pain to be mine and mine yours. I want to rush to help as if you were as important as I, as if your needs were as urgent, as if your mistakes were as innocent. Let us have a single heart, not just a marriage.

I never understood until now why we view the early years of our marriage so differently. You look back on those times as quite unhappy and yet you were the one who was supposedly having all the fun. But dishonesty and betrayal are not fun, regardless of what all the novels and songs say, regardless of the string of new bodies it brought you. Even though your other life was exciting, you were deeply miserable. If you hadn't been you never would have renounced that way so thoroughly.

My friends used to ask me, "How do you stand it? How do you go on?" But I was fairly happy. I had made the decision to forgive you—or else I would not have been—and since I loved you, I simply waited. Even though my friends thought I was being weak, I was really being true to myself. But during that period you were not, and so you were the one they should have been asking, "How do you stand it? How do you go on?"

It's irrelevant to the present how I would like things to have been. How things *are* is the only factor I can deal with. Unless I begin with my life as it is, I am centered in a fantasy. When I find myself blaming, I can be certain I have fallen into this trap. If I see only how you *could* have been, I can blame you. If I see how you are, blame is impossible.

I know how to use my mind to turn away from you. Let me not kid myself that I do not know how to use it to accept you.

The behavior of infidelity may be over, but if we want a real relationship we will have to outendure the unhappy mental dynamic that spawned it. Obviously it will not dissolve with only one or two tries. Without an unshakable commitment to start over again and again, we simply will not become true friends.

Most people hold in their minds such an inflexible picture of how their partner should be that it's impossible for them to make a sincere, sustained effort to join.

Our progress seems hopelessly slow, but we should
be thankful at least that we are willing to try, and
to keep trying without deadline or ultimatum.

Much of life is repetition. Even sex is repetition.
Love is not an emotion, it is a continuous and
irreversible choice. The stage before the eternal
is the recurring.

Revenge is self-defeating. By generating a hate-full self I become self-hating.

I am not my past. I am free. For I am this instant how I choose to be.

Will the struggle be even greater than we thought? I discovered today that we are not numerologically correct. We already knew we were not astrologically correct. And last week in a restaurant that was celebrating the Chinese New Year, I noticed that our animals (you are a pig and I am a goat) are not compatible. So what does this all mean? That we will have to overcome enormous celestial forces that have destroyed most other couples, not to mention animals? I guess we should at least feel a little uncomfortable being a wart on the face of universal law, but I am strangely unworried.

This popular fear that we can lose our identity in another's love for us is not only mistaken but upside down. I know this beyond all doubt when I am with you. Every time I loosen my grip on my own personal importance and sprawl into this puddle of clarity called devotion, I come out brilliantly myself.

Today we will not let the world decide how we feel. We will not get caught up in events and let them dictate our mood. We will not give anything outside ourselves power over our relationship.

Today we are willing to work, willing to start over a thousand times, willing to devote ourselves to this instant only.

Today we will see innocence until we are one.

You and I must work on the mind, not the appearance. Our focus should shift from "How are things between us?" to "How are things within us?" If I want the tone between us to change, I must begin with my own tone. Only the mind can enter heaven. It is the generating point of the *quality* of life. Only the mind can relate. A corpse—a body without a mind—has no relationship.

When does the mind relate? When it is dominated by the embracing emotions: love, acceptance, appreciation, liking, happiness. Whereas the separating emotions—judgment, irritation, discontent, fear— must be withdrawn into; the soul must contract; it must stop relating; it must stop being One.

That little boy with the three-legged dog today—he loved it so much. And the dog loved him. You could see it in his eyes, which never for an instant seemed to leave the boy. Yet the dog could no longer fetch or play rough the way it once could. The boy wanted us to know what a fine dog it had been so we would understand why he still kept it. "My dad asked me if I wanted a new dog for my birthday, but I told him that Max would never understand."

I would rather feel close to you than at one with the stands and pronouncements I have made. I would rather rush to understand, and stumble, than withdraw in perfect virtue and remain upright. I would rather make a thousand offerings to our friendship, and have none returned, than make one empty gesture to my ego. I would rather be happy than right.

You and I have seen the shattered minds and shattered lives that can result from breakups. Often the one most affected is not the one who was left, but the one who took the initiative. There are exceptions, just as there are exceptions to the wisdom of continuing to try, but society kids itself if it believes that people don't pay for their betrayals. The inner toll is so enormous that if a couple could guess at even a portion of the nightmare they are choosing to walk into, they would work a little harder; they would in fact toil.

There is no more powerful, far-reaching, or efficient means of healing than forgiveness, and yet the concept is generally misunderstood. Forgiveness is not a posture of superiority or the decision to behave in certain "forgiving" ways. Forgiveness does not condone the past nor does it commit oneself to the future. It has nothing to do with behaviors such as releasing inmates from the penitentiary or socializing with one's ex-spouse. Forgiveness occurs in the present only. It is my willingness to change my mind from a thing that tortures me into a presence that befriends and comforts me, and this I cannot do as long as I use my mind defensively, or use it to attack. Again and again I must pull thought away from the contemplation of my guilt or yours, back to the recognition of the deep core of innocence that shines within you and every living thing. And this is an effort that must be repeated indefinitely until the soul is healed.

As long as I choose to see you guilty I must remain living proof of what you have done. I must cherish the damage you have caused me and hold tightly to it—for how else will the world stay reminded of your sin?

Whether bodies stay together is meaningless to love. Whether bodies separate is meaningless to freedom. But whether two people turn against each other is everything.

What does it mean to know you? It is acceptance that
leaves room for change but also affirms your unchanging
goodness, your deep perfection. Not as you were, not even
as you are, but as you have always been and always will be.
I am the keeper of your reality.

Sometimes I think that all we are learning in life is that
we are happy when we are kind and unhappy when we are
not. We resist the lesson because it's so simple it's
insulting.

I have always been comfortable around you. But what is it about comfort that I and so many others feel we must run from in terror? In our culture why is it made out to be the destroyer of initiative and creativity? Comfort is merely the door to the peace of God, but it must be opened.

It seems that the whole world hurts more these days. The lives of most of my friends are painful to look at. And when I try to help I usually make matters worse. But all pain slips away when you laugh. And in the light of your smile I can relax.

Funny how the world grows softer when I remember to love you.

All that our friend Marie wanted was to go back to school and get her degree. But Steve kept reminding her that they had decided years ago that college was a waste of time and money, that the most creative thinking was coming from people who were outside of traditional education. And so a marriage of eleven years between two honorable people broke up, leaving two confused and unhappy young children, and two adults who were now free to have it their own way.

Nothing more is needed than to choose a way for your mind to be happy now. When happiness is your decision, you have begun the path that will lead you out of any pain.

"Love is blind" means that love is happy being itself. Love can even grow without being returned. It is this quality that makes love invulnerable.

About the only time people pay close attention to under-
wear is when they are buying it. So that it will appear
smooth for that one moment, the rough side of the
stitching is turned under where only the body it covers
can tell. Likewise the soft side of the flannel in shirts
and pajamas is on the outside. Even the seam of a comb
is hidden between its teeth so that it will appear
smooth and easy on the hair. In the world, appearance
is everything.

It is enough that individuals look successful, that couples
seem in love, that governments image righteousness.
Every morning throughout the world people leave
their homes with their bodies in order, and their minds
in disarray. It's not as if millions don't know some way
of ordering their minds and centering themselves within
their hearts, but they think they don't have time. Yet
they find time to put on both shoes and all their clothes,
to groom their bodies and void their bowels. They have
time to go forth *presentable,* but not time to go forth in
a kind and helpful state of mind.

The usual means of selecting one's mate is no less dominated by appearances. Those seen as ordinary are not considered. But if the calves are a centimeter higher, if the eyes are a centimeter wider, if the clothes come from the right store, if the career gives the right impression, if the accent is from the right part of the country, if the age is less and the hair is more, then the individual is attractive and desirable and worthy of all-consuming, single-minded pursuit. No one would be so dumb as to pick a friend because he or she had good legs, and yet considerations such as that influence the choice of one's life partner. What comfort is a complexion when you must come home and tell of a business failure? What tenderness and fun can the right height give to your newborn child? And in illness what compassion can come from net worth? Looks good or *is* good: that is the needed shift in perception.

People think nothing of devoting a year to learning a new sport, two years to learning a new language, decades to getting the degrees they want, and half a century to reach the top of their profession. But somehow a great love should fall unbidden from the stars. The current belief is that if a couple has to work at it, they are not soul mates. In fact, they are probably departing from the Plan just in seeing each other. If they continually have to start over and settle for a little gain each day, either they lack all knowledge of metaphysics, are working out bad Karma, or one of them is a new soul and a shoddy one at that.

What is the sacrifice if friendship grows? What
is given up if love fills the void?

It was not until we started accepting each other
as if we had been picked to be together by all the
angels in heaven that we began to experience an
arranged marriage.

Most couples focus on what is lacking. Within the heart, within the soul, nothing is lacking.

To be in love is merely to focus your full attention on love.

take my hand
but more than this
take my heart, and give me yours
    that I may love
you even more than with one
heart alone

a single life takes such little
caring for
give me your needs
    that I may strive for more than mine
give me your wounds
    that I may be a healer
give me your dreams
    that I may work miracles

for if I treat you well
from the insufficiencies of my being
I will pull forth light
    and know myself
        as light in you

You drive me crazy when you get absentminded. I see you standing there with that glazed look in your eyes, insisting that you didn't put the cheese under the sink, that you don't know how the mail got into the dishwasher, and of course I know this little trait can be thought of as endearing and that if we are ever to have peace on earth we must first have peace in our kitchens. But what you don't realize is that I come from a line of people who not only never misplaced their keys but also were willing to kill small animals to maintain order. This is how they helped society evolve in a positive direction, whereas you are the invasion of the Mongols. Only a ravaging barbarian would set the iron down on the carpet because the phone was ringing.

Why do you bring things up just as we're going to bed? You would rather argue than sleep, and if I show any signs of weariness you get furious. In your family they scream at each other and throw things against the wall. In my family they never raise their voice, they just get divorced. I don't want a divorce, I just want to pretend that everything is okay until morning. Our relationship may be a sham, but a rested sham is better than a tired one.

If it were sex I was proposing, you would be all ears —or some other organ. If I were throwing my clothes against the wall, you would join right in. I wouldn't mind waiting until morning if you hadn't been suggesting that ploy for ten years. *No* sham is better than a rested one.

Often in the heat of an argument I have seen the point-lessness of it all, or have suddenly wanted us to be close rather than this, or have felt a surge of generosity. And I can remember similar impulses on your part. We each seem to have moments of fairness, it's just that they don't come at the same time. Apologies are not accepted but used as an invitation to unveil a new list of grievances, compromises are never seen as enough, and a sincere desire to do better is taken as a sign of weakness. If we could somehow reorganize our arguments so that the times of goodwill coincided, we would come away encouraged rather than disheartened.

Let's use our knowledge of each other in a different way. We know how to hurt each other, how to humiliate and make each other angry. We know just what to say and do. Now let's take these same intuitions and learn to use them to make each other happy.

I asked Mark why he carries a picture of Kimberly when she was eight. "When I get mad at her," he said, "I pull this out and remember a time when she was innocent."

If an argument merely serves each party's separate interests, it is but one battle in a campaign to establish dominance. Except that dominance cannot be established. Some animals appear to accept it, but there is a part of the human mind that feels its equality with all others, and I have never known an adult or a child who on a very deep level did not instinctively reject dominance as an assault on truth. Arguments, as they are usually conducted, go against our basic nature and quite naturally lead nowhere.

Most arguments are little more than verbal attack.
The minds are heated and very defensive. For two
people to state plainly what they want is a way of
cutting through criticism and accusations and as such
can be a step in the direction of love. But just as a
demand is a more honest form of communication than
a criticism, a genuine expression of one's fears is
more basic still. The mind must begin to go inward in
order to recognize its fears. A criticism is a
description of you, a demand is a description of myself
in relation to you, whereas an acknowledgment of
fear is primarily a description of myself and therefore
tends to trigger less defensiveness in you.

Behind every want is a fear that is father to it. When in the course of an argument the fears are individually seen and released, very little remains to prevent the individuals from joining. If only the wants or demands are voiced, fear, which is the more disruptive layer, is left essentially untouched. Each fear must be brought to conscious attention or else it will merely take form in other wants at other times.

It is easier to let go of a fear than a want. That is the key. As we have been practicing stating our positions in terms of what we are afraid of rather than what we want, I notice that when I see your genuine apprehensions and doubts, I truly desire to help. And when I am quiet long enough to recognize what I myself am afraid of—and not just reword my criticisms using the word "fear"—I am more willing to be done with it, and done with it now.

I noticed a peculiar attitude yesterday when you
were telling me your side of this question about the
amniocentesis test, and I realized that it's an
attitude that is usually prevalent between any two
who are arguing without love. I was listening to you
as if you didn't mean what you were saying. It was
as though you were making up your ideas just to be
perverse. No one could be that wrong and still mean
it. When I admitted to myself that of course you did mean
it, a remarkably strong effort was necessary to keep my
mind from drifting back into the "you're just being
difficult" attitude. The result, as might be expected,
was that at last I *saw* your position, and a way out of
our impasse followed very quickly.

We have within us two ways of hearing: one comes from the body and is sensitive to anything that is different from it, the other comes from the point of joining and is sensitive to anything that affects unity. One hears in parts and pieces, the other hears in wholes.

Words were made to designate differences. They are small and hard and do not easily wrap around the deeper sensibilities. To hold you to your words shuts me off from the stream of feelings you are trying to describe. I cannot hear you with my ears, but only with my heart.

There is an inner state that permits a lovely and healing form of spontaneity, but estrangement, disaffection, and righteousness can only bring forth their own kind. Thus a spontaneous argument (one with no guidelines) puts the relationship at great risk because the friendship is not intact as the argument begins. Here, awareness and great care are needed rather than spontaneity, or at the least a procedure that will allow these to enter as the discussion proceeds.

"Go with the flow" assumes a state peaceful enough to see what the flow is. Spontaneity is neither good nor bad; it simply means that I am choosing to act directly out of whatever attitudes are presently dominating my mind. It is only as productive as the mental state from which it springs.

Always be aware of what the ego is up to. No effort should be spared to bring every negative thought and emotion into full consciousness. But to acknowledge and accept the personal nature of our ego does not mean we must identify with it as our only self. We have surprisingly little control over our ego—and to endlessly battle it only strengthens its grip on our mind—but we are free to return our thoughts to peace, which is our basic nature, any instant we so choose.

We each have strengths but we use them to attack the other's areas of vulnerability. We use our humor to put down, our fearlessness to mock, our intelligence to confound, and our knowledge of each other's sensitivities to defeat. When we respect the other's weaknesses, as we have been trying to do recently, each weakness in one is balanced by a strength in the other. This has nothing to do with traditional sex roles but rather with the fact that all egos are different and that it is rare for two individuals to have shortcomings in identical areas. This is as true with broad attributes as with minor aptitudes. You have a deep sense of direction that can keep us on course, and I know how to step more lightly and easily over the difficulties that strew the path. You are better on the telephone and protect me from needless upset by making all business calls. I am a better driver and we are all happier when you are on the passenger side. Honest acceptance of our differences allows our relationship to function like a single body. The left hand is in a better position to reach certain objects than the right and vice versa. The legs are well suited for functions that the arms are not. There is no war between limbs because the body is united by a single purpose, a single heart.

There is no perfect plan for how to argue. Perhaps
it's enough that there be an agreed-upon approach.
However, there would seem to be certain obvious
fundamentals: Choosing a time that is conducive to
concentration. Not taking up more than can be
solved. Listening. Being fair. And possibly more
than all else, using arguing as a means of helping the
friendship. When you and I argue with awareness—
awareness of the direction we want our friendship to go—
we benefit far more by improving the marriage
we both live in than we ever could by merely making
a point or extracting acquiescence.

During an argument I have an inner option: to honor your ego or your self, to feel your reactions or your goodness, to see you as a threat or as my friend. During an argument my pettiness has already been called to, so it will take an effort to recall that, should I choose to hear it out, there is something in me that knows you better than my anger.

Although the heart guides quite specifically, we have never had a difference when we have turned to our hearts. It is impossible for Love to give conflicting advice.

I think a time comes when a couple longs to go beyond "getting it all out." It's true that loud emotional arguments often leave us feeling numb, drained, and "finished." They can even lead to good sex. But we are both noticing now that these flare-ups, although much more infrequent, are taking longer to get over. Even a slight tear in the heart causes deep anguish. I think we both want the kind of peace that cannot be broken. We no longer wish to take time out from happiness to hurt each other, even a little.

The body and the time one has are worn out by these constant battles with the imperfection of everything. We don't think we have time to relax into our life *as it is.* We don't think we have time to enjoy our house or our children or our garden. But a monstrous quantity of time is spent fighting the house, fighting the ways of children, fighting the grass and the plants.

The ego is always doing what it does not need to be doing *now.*

Anxiety is a desire to do what is not necessary.
When looked at correctly, anxiety is a form of
intuitive knowing, not of what will happen, but
of what would be a senseless battle.

We have time. In a sense, time is the only thing
the world has to offer. And devotion to whatever
is before us now is the key to its pleasant use.

This morning, after working on the stain for three minutes, John said, "It won't come up." I worked on it half an hour and it came up.

Accompanying the present widespread belief in magic, "guidance," and special powers is the unavoidable conclusion that if an effort must be repeated, something has gone wrong: "If it doesn't flow, let it go." The couple from the workshop said, "We tried your way of arguing Saturday night and it doesn't work." The usual attitude we have toward our lives is that repeating the same *mistake* is only natural: "After all, we're only human; we all have our limitations." The couple had argued unsuccessfully many times, and will continue to do so, but they thought nothing of quitting after one application of an answer.

The distaste and resistance we feel to "giving into" our partner is greater than most of us admit. It is more than a fear of imprisonment; it is almost a fear of dying. Consequently we think we must never apologize with all of our heart. And if we acquiesce we must do so begrudgingly. Because the simple fact is that we do not *want* to understand our partner's position, we do not *want* to discover how much it means to him or her, we do not *want* to know what relief our acceptance might bring. We would rather stick coldly to our point than experience the humiliation of warmth.

In a world that values effortless relating, to make the effort to commit to loving another individual throughout a long life together is as brave a deed as climbing Mount Everest, scaling the barbed-wire fence of a nuclear power plant, or giving up a posh job to work with the homeless. And surely the measure of comfort it brings to the world is equally great.

Issues over diet, TV, and video games are tearing apart many potentially excellent parental teams, and all in the name of what is "best" for the child! The greatest gift we can give our children is our willingness to work through our problems. And if the outcome is a child who believes in the possibility of love, who can calculate the effect?

John was the model new-age child. He was nice, quiet, said spiritual things to guests, and had long eyelashes. People asked us how we did it. And we told them. Evidently the Karma Police were listening, because they sent us Jordan. Last night we finally admitted the basic feeling we both have: We got the wrong child. It's as if there was a cosmic mix-up and somewhere there's a mother saying, "What's wrong with him? He never screams! He never hits nobody! He just lies there and smiles." She got our baby.

Jordan's behavior is affecting both of us. Since he's only two we can't kid ourselves that he has developed a powerful shadow side of which we are the victim. It must be something we are doing, and the fact that we did not bond with him when he was born must be reversed. If we can eat three times a day, we can surely pause quietly three times a day to open our hearts to Jordan. A two-year-old cannot accommodate. It is we who must deeply accept him. Certainly we want to be firm when firmness is called for, but firmness is not anger. With a little child, unconditional love is not an option, it is a necessity.

The opposite of being nice to someone, and one sure way of making matters worse, is trying to get someone to be nice to us—through guilt. And yet in dealing with one's child or one's mate, this is standard practice.

The primary function of a parent is not correction but friendship.

Give your approval *before* your child asks for it.

So many of us today merely stress another set of external values while continuing to fail our children on the same deep level our parents failed us. Before, a clean "well-kept" child was considered a loved child, and its preparation for life was believed assured by teaching it to be polite and to work hard at school. Children were thought protected because the neighborhoods, and even many of the towns, were safe from kidnappers and molesters. Although their parents stayed married, the true grounds for affection, preparation, and protection were missing because children were not provided a deeply unified and loving home. They were surrounded by dishonest examples of devotion and therefore grew up to be openly disloyal.

Instead of, "Keep your nose clean and remember your manners," our advice today is more likely to be, "Don't play with war toys. Don't eat white sugar. Don't watch *GI Joe*." And even though we are now free to change partners endlessly, we are not providing our children with an atmosphere of connectedness and enduring kindness in which to flourish. We have changed the issues, but we are still using them to keep from concentrating on the *true* health and happiness of our children.

We are working very hard to learn how to relate to this new computer. We must work equally hard to learn how to relate to each of our boys individually. One is no less an acquired skill than the other.

To *discipline* out of anger or fear merely teaches children that we value anger and fear more than love and therefore so should they. True firmness is based on love, and love is felt as the firmness is being exercised.

We have been having these daily meditation sessions on Jordan for four months now and the results could not have been more unexpected. We thought we would merely come to accept and like him, and that has happened, but suddenly Jordan has blossomed. Actually, we are not sure if he has changed or if we are seeing him clearly for the first time. Now he is highly inventive, mentally tough, and has a nonstop humor that refreshes the whole family. Tonight, as I was putting him to bed, I asked him what he thought about God. He said, "I don't like him. He keeps me awake at night and has a weird name."

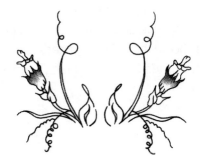

Dear Son,

Every child brings a unique blessing. I knew this, of course, but for two years I thought yours was so unique as to be mostly invisible. Because if we as expectant parents are honest, most of us will admit to wanting a special child, but special within the bounds of "wonderful." Your gift is a deep honesty that thinks nothing of telling monumental lies about how much candy was eaten and when teeth were brushed but cannot abide the kind of phony niceness that veils parental insensitivity. You will dismember the contents of several rooms to make one of your "engines," and yet you will practice many long minutes to perfect a face that makes us all laugh. You hate your very spiritual kindergarten, but you love to come back home and cannot understand why any of us should ever be apart. You will swear with shocking abandon and yet you are consistently gentle and patient with other children, even in the face of their rejection. I've never seen you take on anyone who wasn't bigger than you. Most of us have become so accustomed to betraying our deepest selves that we no longer have a sense of our true identity, but even in the face of early rejection you never did. I've watched you refuse to answer the kind of patronizing questions adults often ask children, until they are looking at you with anxious foreboding and talking about cats getting people's tongues. And I squirm with them because it's so much "nicer" for a mother to have a child who answers. There are many times when I wish I could make life easier for you, but I honor your courage and your purity. And I thank God daily that you came to be with us.

Children hear moods more loudly than words.

Excessive reasoning or explanation almost always
has behind it the belief that guilt can be a tool.

This incessant battle with John and Jordan over
language they are picking up in the neighborhood is
violating a basic lesson. We know every word they
know, and experience has taught us when not to use
them. Yet we are acting as if this bit of wisdom
will somehow escape them in life. Here is what we
must return to: Never react to children out of fear
of what they might become. Base your decisions on
your present perception of what will serve their
happiness and peace today.

Our third night in L.A. found us having—not an argument, we are too advanced for that—but a protracted in-depth discussion. John kept coming to us and saying, "You're tired. Why don't you just go to bed." But he's only seven and doesn't understand adults' deep need to be miserable at night. Realizing that his tactic was not going to work, he finally came to us and said, "Why don't you sit down and ask God." Well! We couldn't easily ignore that, since we had been giving him similar advice all his life. So we sat down and closed our eyes, and God said, "You're tired. Why don't you just go to bed." I guess sometimes adults become so outrageous that kids just have to blow their cover.

Dear Son,

So often parents think of their children as failing investments whose cost in time and money outweighs the return. Whenever I find myself thinking of you in this way, I picture God looking at me.

Here we are doing a workshop at Omega during "Family Week" and Jordan is keeping us honest. There must be a hundred kids, and since all the workshops for their parents are about them, naturally they are acting out every form of questionable behavior imaginable. One of the Gasses' older children got up on the faculty dining table, lay down, and started sucking her thumb. And when the McMahons, the editors of *Mothering* magazine whom we have been wanting to meet for several years, came over, Jordan pulled my head down, right in the middle of my overly nice conversation with Peggy, and whispered in my ear, "You are a ba-gina sucking pig." I was so shocked that all I could do was smile and whisper back, "It's *va*-gina."

The new couple down the block have an eleven-year-old they call their "special-ed son." They see him as the point at which their life went awry. The central focus of their relationship with him is to have him progress to where he can get his driver's license and live in an apartment by himself "without causing too much trouble." They don't understand that they can also love him and deeply accept him *as he is now,* and still work toward these goals. For him to cooperate with their present motivation would be to sanction their pushing him away, so of course he does not cooperate. And because they don't *see* him, they are blind to the boundless pleasure he could give.

God halts childhood at age nine and says, "You think you have it figured out so I want you to see a little preview of adolescence." John is unquestionably going through this, and I notice that you and I have been slipping into the role of the ugly parent. *Most of the time parents give to their children is spent correcting them.* Even in amusement parks or on playgrounds—where the ostensible purpose is fun— there is frequently a slight underlying tone of irritation, censure, or patronization. Certainly parents must be firm at times, but what children need more than constant vigilance is an unfaltering supporter, one who assumes their basic goodness and knows absolutely how they will turn out. They need a friend who is wiser and older and sees their mistakes and weaknesses, but even while correcting unhappy behavior, holds them up to the light of their own being. Their playmates, teachers, coaches, etc., cannot confer this basic faith. Only the parent is in a position to give the gift of self-worth permanently.

When you suggested that one Saturday each month we have either a Jordan Day or John Day, both of us were not only happy with the plan, we were excited. This reaction makes no sense from an ego standpoint. Children's idea of fun is different from adults' and so why would spending all day doing what a five-year-old or nine-year-old wanted strike us as wonderful? When we look back we can see that many of our happiest moments have been those times like Christmas, birthdays, or even a crisis, when we have devoted ourselves completely to one of our children or to each other. We have often remarked that it's even better for the one giving the good day than for the one receiving it. And how often we have heard parents in our grief group say that the happiest period of their lives was the time they devoted to their dying child. Yet the resistance we all feel to this ancient idea is enormous. Even though the sentiment would be a thousand times more valid, it would probably irritate most people if instead of saying, "Have a good day," one were to say, "Give someone a good day."

We did it again. We were going to drive to Sebastopol and ended up in Seattle. Now there are excuses to be made to schoolteachers, to publishers, and to friends who were not informed. I don't think any of us wanted the trip to end. Why is it the whole family, even the dog, is quite happy driving great distances together? Although to hear us complain about the smelly motels, aching backs, the antics of other drivers, and the food, no one would believe it. We say we are glad to get home, but actually we are a little sad the torture is over. I think it's because on the road a simple life is forced on us. There is really nothing else to concentrate on except how we are treating each other. There are no bills, no pressing errands, no particular schedule that must be followed. All the rules become flexible. The minutiae that always seem to get between us are swept away by endless highways. Nothing remains to compete for our love for each other. Nor should one duty or need ever be allowed back in that position.

May this home be a welcome within Your open arms.
May it be a reflection of the Home we have never left.
We will honor one another as Your gift and sacred trust.
We will speak gently to each other, as You have spoken to us.
We will look with eyes that cherish, as Your eyes cherish all.
We want no mood but understanding,
No attitude but peace.
If we are everything You want,
Let us also be everything we want,
As we wake in You, at home in You, forever.

Because the picture that the body presents seems more important to us than the acts of our heart, we believe that it is a part of kindness to join the sad in their sadness, to join the angry in their anger, to join the depressed in their depression. But we do not take on another's burden in this way. When we flood our heart with any emotion that is less than the innermost splendor of the one who is before us, we blind ourselves to what is needed and what could help.

To give understanding we must continue to understand. To give love we must continue *being* loving. To give a hand to another we must grasp firmly the only hand that has ever held us.

Last night, while we were listening to one more couple fight, it struck me how obtuse we all are. As have most other couples, they have had fights like that a hundred times before—without ever questioning the exercise of fighting itself. They were working very hard. They were concentrating. They were intent. Obviously they still had hope that this time attack would work.

If you judge it, it still controls you.

I will let this day come to me and bring me peace.

Many couples today are getting "a friendly divorce," as if that were an end in itself. But the thought that caused them to separate remains a driving force in their lives, and it will apply to each new relationship until the thought itself is questioned.

When love is finally valued for itself, and no longer thought of as a means of attracting, holding, or manipulating other people, happiness will abide, regardless of what scene is before the eyes.

So much of relationships is running after what
you don't have and when it turns toward you, bolting
off. In the world, all value is based on scarcity.
Consequently, in most marriages there is one who
chases and one who backs away. When either
decides not to play his or her role, a crisis in value
is precipitated. Value, however, does not lie in
inequality. It lies in deep mutual respect—which
is not earned but given.

It takes time to dislike. As I walk into the house, it takes an additional moment to dislike the tile, and this bit of mental poison is carried into the next activity and affects it. But notice that I don't do anything about the tile. To replace the tile would be one way to renounce disliking it, and there are many other ways. But my choice is merely to dislike it. Dislike is a pointless and inconsistent activity. Days, weeks go by in which the tile has been driven from my mind by some other concern. During this time the tile is seen but not disliked.

Liking isn't the opposite of disliking, unless it's merely a taking of sides, a conceit, a pridefulness. Liking is simple enjoyment, and this good, restful state of mind is an easy atmosphere in which devotion can thrive.

Although some of the emotions generated during the infatuation stage of a relationship are dishonest, the mind's much-overlooked ability to decline each judgmental thought as it arises is amply demonstrated. It's not that the two don't see each other's faults and limitations, but they instantly dismiss them because they *want* to fall in love and instinctively know that to dwell on any criticism would kill the mood. Later in the relationship, never is it true that things have "gone too far," because this same ability to reject unloving thoughts can be used at any time. The ability is not "seeing no evil," but not cherishing the other's mistakes as his or her basic reality.

Our neighbors called again to complain about noise. Our immediate reaction was anger. But immediate reactions rarely lead to peace or even resolution of the problem. Our assumption is that they have a choice. And we condemn them for failing to exercise it. But we know from our own unhappy histories that until a certain level of learning is reached, until "the light has gone on," they do *not* have a choice. They are simply acting out a personality type whose reality we are free to acknowledge or deny. When we indulge in disapproval, we are not "being ourselves," but merely joining them in the mistake. Action may be called for, but censure is a lapse in intelligence that we don't allow ourselves even with our own pets. We would not condemn our cat for being too aloof or our dog for not being aloof enough, because we know they have no choice. If the neighbors were a family of baboons who hung out the windows and shouted gibberish at us, we might be appalled, but not angry. It is up to us, not them, to see their innocence.

To minds trained in judgment, an innocent vision
seems weak. I stand at the threshold of your
innocence and know not how to respond. I have only
learned how to get irritated and attack back. The
only difference between us is that I have experienced,
a little, the freedom and grandeur of seeing without
guilt. And I know that it is possible to act forcefully
in any situation and still not judge it. And so I am
determined that I will not lose myself in your fire
and anger. To do so would defeat us both. And more
than that, it would break the fragile thread of
oneness that is our inheritance.

Last week, for some reason, I suddenly couldn't stand the whole family. And what's more, I couldn't be bothered explaining it. I just stuck my head in a book all day and refused to help out. I hope all of you know the gift you gave me by not reacting—and then never mentioning it.

Dear Son,

Thank you for believing I should be your pal
when I thought I was too old.
Thank you for teaching me to fish
when I thought I was too moral.
Thank you for sharing your RC's
when I thought I had sworn off caffeine.
Thank you for taking me roller skating
when I thought I was too brittle.
Thank you for telling me your nightmares
when I thought I had to sleep.
Thank you for teaching me what the fingers mean
when I thought I already knew.
Thank you for showing me your scabs, for taking me
to baseball card shops, for making me box without
hitting back, for inviting me to sit beside you when
you watched *Inspector Gadget*.
Thank you, Son, for somehow knowing I was capable
of being your dad.

If Mother had only known the pain Bill would go through after she died, she would have stopped smoking instantly. Perhaps I can redeem her mistake with this pledge to you. Because I don't want you to worry, I will eat more sensibly. Because I don't want you to know fear, I will drive with more awareness. Because I don't want you to feel jealousy, I will dress with more compassion. Because I don't want to shatter your tranquility, I will not misunderstand so quickly. Truly, I want to be a comfort in your life, not a source of distress. And above all I want you to know the peace of God. Therefore, I will at least *try* to weigh the effects of everything I do, of every word I speak, of every line of thought I pursue. If I am your friend, how could I do less?

Why do you love me even though I'm fat?

It's true you are fat. And perhaps I could woo a younger,
slimmer body. But that body would come with a younger,
slimmer mind. Your mind does not offer the shallow
excitement of an unopened package. It is the gift itself,
a spring of clear water in which I can wash away all my
confusions and loneliness.

If you truly loved me you would guess what I want you to do in bed without my having to tell you. If you truly loved me you would know my body as though it were your own and I would not have to make these embarrassing requests. It would be like walking on a mirror, or playing with my shadow, or answering an echo. . . . Well, on second thought, please remain hopelessly confused.

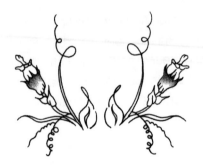

So many of the older couples we are seeing have turned away from each other. Their bodies have become reminders of age and death, and they can no longer gaze at each other with the total appreciation they once had. Even a kiss on a now wrinkled cheek is vaguely difficult. Compliments—that once were so spontaneously given—now must be asked for. And, if given at all, physical affection is somewhat forced and self-conscious. *It does not have to be this way.* Because the attitude is different, in many areas of life age is thought to be the bringer of beauty: weathered wood, antique brick, ancient trees, old family homes, the patina of a masterpiece. Our choice of what within us looks determines what we see. And to see and touch with love can be practiced and relearned.

A honeymoon is a strange concept. It is supposed to
be the sweetest part of the venture, when it's new,
when there is much to uncover. And once uncovered, I
am left with what? A half-moon? How foolish I was
to have thought I could have loved you more when I
did not know you.

Certainly sex can be "I will do that for you if you
will do this for me," but what a lonely arrangement.
A caress should say "I love you," not pay off a debt.
An embrace should fill the heart as well as the arms.

Bodies can tell a tale that ideas cannot master and words cannot convey. At first our bodies spoke excitedly and anxiously to each other because they understood very little of love's language, and it's funny to realize that these few marked-off moments could be considered "the high points of a relationship." In the years since, we have gradually engendered a sex *life* that extends into ordinary gestures and words and adds a warm gentleness to our days. Now our bodies relate a sweet, quiet story that no bed need start and no sensation need end.

Your partner can offer you but one thing,
the opportunity to choose peace.

If you're going to leave the decision up to your
partner, don't find fault with it.

At any given time one partner is stronger than the other, and it is up to that person to remember his or her debt of gratitude to the other. Ordinarily this role passes back and forth, but when we pointed out to the group that you singlehandedly carried our marriage for twelve years, many people were shocked and did not understand how that was possible. You answered that what you did was never to stop loving me. I think that what you did *not* do is equally crucial. You did not focus on my behavior. You did not become preoccupied with how you were being treated. Instead you worked hard on your own spiritual growth. In this way you were able to gently turn aside your friends' well-meant assurances that you deserved better, as well as your parents' intimations that the situation was somehow your fault. You have shown me and many others a priceless option: *any* life situation can become my path—if I respond to it with gentleness.

We have within us two guides, the ego and the heart.
A successful couple is one that has learned not to
consult the ego on what the *purpose* of the relationship
is, in other words, on what the partner should or
should not be doing, on what the partner looks like,
on where the partner is headed, on what the partner
has done that must be paid for. The successful
couple knows that the ego always speaks first and
therefore waits for this reaction to pass and a quiet
knowledge to take its place.

Most parents can change a diaper and still see their baby as pure and lovable. They don't even hear their ego's opinion of the sight and smell. When their child makes its first drawings, they don't consult their ego opinion of art. They are not critical of how a hug is given or of how the breath smells in the morning. They bypass the voice of their ego altogether and listen instead to the lovely wisdom of their heart. Any adult can learn to look upon his or her mate with similar fairness, although great practice is usually required.

The body does not have to be given free rein to act out every passing mood. The reflexive repetition of lifelong patterns is not "free," but a deeply unconscious approach to life. Changing the mind-set to a more helpful state can be facilitated by changing the statement the body is making to the mind. The body is like a dream, which seems to run its course independently of the mind and to dictate the state the mind is in. But just as a dream or fantasy can be "guided" to heal the mind, so the body can be guided to conform to a more profound layer of being and reflect back to the mind its deeper desires.

Choice can represent the lower level of experience in which one's self and all living things seem separate, unalike, and unloved, or the higher level of experience in which the unity of life is felt and the common interests of all are known. There is undoubtedly a sense of happiness that comes from self-indulgence, but it's often overlooked that another kind of pleasure accompanies a higher effort. To walk simply and directly toward one's heart goal is to know a happiness that can be shared, and at least glimpse the one happiness that will last.

Like a monkey chattering in a tree, the ego judges everything that passes below it. From its imagined height it can see no equality, no innocence. It is always a mistake to fight against this sound. To do so merely makes its voice seem more real.

Another sound must be heard in addition. At first it will be very faint, present one moment, then vanishing quite arbitrarily. But as it is listened for consistently, it gradually takes possession of the heart, and even the clatter of the ego becomes a source of amusement, and problems, large and numerous as before, are not magically swept away, but are seen clearly, and now can be lightly stepped over, each and every one. From within, this will look like dancing.

Let love begin simply as your life,
the thing you take for granted, the ground you walk on.
Love must cease to be a supplement to the real
and become reality itself, which it always was.

Like a low lovely hum,
    you must sense it always in the background.
Like the soft ringing of bells on the wind,
    you must *feel* the sound.
Like a heartbeat of the mind,
    you must know it is always there.

Keep your attention divided,
for no matter what else is before you,
love must be behind you lifting you up,
carrying you away, and dissolving every concern,
every purpose you have
but love.

We counseled another new couple and have made the same mistake again. When they left they were as content as baked potatoes and we have been at each other ever since. Our words and reactions are not the same as theirs, but the underlying attitudes are identical. The ego will always mimic whatever it believes is real. It's unreasonable for us to think that just because we know better we are not going to pick up some of what we come in contact with. We must quickly let go of it or stop counseling altogether if we wish to protect our friendship. For what is the overall gain if the problem dies in them but lives on in us?

These times are very difficult on relationships, but we do not have to be a product of our times. We do not need the same problems we read about, or uncover in counseling, or see our friends go through.

It once was a struggle to get divorced; now it's a struggle to stay together, and those who do are charting new territory. It is the great experiment of our times. Couples now must stay together because they want to, because they are devoted to forming a real friendship and will let nothing in their lives come before that goal.

A sense of oneness is very fragile. We must not treat it casually. It is in fact the sacred trust of our era, because all who have it are guardians of the only candle that can light a way through the world's pall of loneliness and loss.

When a good relationship is exposed to the ill will of the world, one feels the cynicism as if it were one's own, and thus the tendency is for true friends to view the strength of their unity with the same distaste that some others view it. Although they may do so unconsciously, the miserable can work quite hard to pull everyone else into misery. You and I must protect what we have labored so hard to develop. We must not talk about our happiness unnecessarily, or through our behavior needlessly draw attention to our devotion. Yet we must also remember that nothing can affect the bond between us unless we make it important and take it into our hearts as a reality, as a truth. Even if it's a couple we are trying to help, in order for us to be harmed, we must elevate the appearance of their separateness and subordinate the fact of our oneness.

To watch two people fight, to feel their mutual dislike, to see them in the process of failing at what they once wanted so deeply, imposes a powerful picture on our minds. In effect it is a pictorial lie of separation as the basic reality. Yet only if we accept their belief in discord as sufficient evidence that oneness is unreal can we be affected. Only if we forget what we have experienced can we be influenced to turn against each other. Nevertheless, we must honestly face our tendency to do just that.

The ancient practice of surrounding in light is surprisingly effective. I can't be affected by another's negativity if I don't fear it or judge it. Often there is a part of my mind that sees the other person quite clearly, but my tendency is to turn a genuine insight into a judgment and for my mind to do this so quickly that the shift from light to dark goes unnoticed. Surrounding in light retraces my mental steps and releases the poison without eliminating the insight.

We went into that little store on the plaza to buy
your dad some slippers and the salesman had not
spoken ten words before we caught each other's eye,
thanked him nicely, and left. Even though he had been
outwardly polite, we both sensed that he was angry
and miserable, at least for that afternoon. But
instead of fighting a useless battle, as we would
have a few years ago, we simply removed ourselves
from the atmosphere. I think we have finally learned
never to put the peace between us in jeopardy.

These periods we have been setting aside each day
to surround certain people in light, helping in a way
we *can* help, are deeply satisfying, if not self-healing.
But I am convinced that if we started talking carelessly
about these efforts or if we became curious
about the results, our peace would gradually give way
to anxiety. These gifts must be pure, without sin,
without calculation. Nevertheless, the feeling is
palpable that even though no change may be observed,
an effect occurs on a deeper level, the same benefit
that we ourselves receive.

There were those years I had to live in a separate house just to keep from leaving you, and now, twenty years later, I receive such peace and strength by having you near that when you are away even a few hours I begin functioning in the world less efficiently, and certainly less happily. When I first began noticing this I became frightened that I was developing a weakening dependency, but now as I look at the state I slip into I see that it's merely a return to normal—the normal human feeling of being alone in the world. Perhaps the time will come when I will know rather than just believe that we carry each other in our hearts, but for now I will settle for peace from proximity.

I don't cope very well with people. Trying to relate
exhausts me because when I open my mouth I never
know what's going to come out. All I know is that if
you are there, one person at least will not hold it
against me.

Thank you for knowing me well enough that nothing I
say or do can revise your opinion of me.

For the last few weeks, whenever we have been together in the car, I have been practicing what I have come to call "divine gossip." Before, I always thought you were being small-minded and unspiritual, but since trying to participate (which has required that I listen to you more carefully) I see that you merely find people fascinating and that there is really no malice in you. An even more surprising discovery is that in the past, when I would call for silence, I was not using the silence for anything but a kind of withdrawn idle thinking. There is more love, and therefore more depth, in my gossiping with you than in "thinking great thoughts" by myself.

This experiment of trying to like what the other one likes has taught me to approach my ego indirectly. I can't just say, "Now I will like to shop," or, "Now I will like to chat while driving," without triggering resistance. I have to find my particular way of enjoying it. Or more to the point, I have to find a specific selfish way of being unselfish. When I started looking at clothing stores as modern museums, that was a breakthrough. Then I bought *Woman's Wear Daily,* since here are writers who believe that fashion is interesting. To think that there could be an international war over hemlines and that the Americans would feel betrayed by the French! I find that shop owners will talk to me with no small emotion about this perfidy. So I am not following you into stores but into battle zones. Now that is something a man can get interested in.

This week I took the final step. I tuned in K-PIG.
Your jaw actually dropped. "What did you do that
for?" "Well," I said, "I just wanted to see what
you listen to when I'm not here." An hour later I
found myself wondering if Perlman or Zuckerman
could keep up with the best of the bluegrass
fiddlers. And the lyrics were *beyond* comparison:
"If you want to keep your beer real cold, hold it
against my ex-wife's heart," or, "My head hurts, my
feet stink, and I don't love Jesus." Here is a whole
new way of singing about misery.

An opinion, being pre-set, blocks ideas that may be needed now.

In some major areas of taste, areas that I thought before were untouchable, I have come to like what you like. This raises to doubt the sacred idol of personal differences. What value is there in having two egos when one will do?

Even though our opinions change constantly, even though we are capable of believing what no one else believes, even though we cringe at the opinions we once upheld, still we defend the opinions we have today as if the sanctity of our identity depended on them, and we can feel personally attacked if someone disagrees.

As I go through the day I have been saying, "Gayle is everything I want and everything I need. Her opinions are mine. I want no separate opinions. Her longings and tastes, her wishes and concerns, all are mine. I have no desire, and there is no reason, to contrast myself with Gayle." This exercise has been surprisingly freeing and has brought me great peace. And yet I suspect that for many people it would be a detrimental approach. It is possible here because you have no history of needing to control as I have had, and you are also very intelligent and pure, so I run no risk of subjugating myself to some quality that is dark or destructive. Nevertheless, it's interesting how little ego is needed to function in the world and how many useless battles are eliminated by refusing to be right.

Love is a way of thinking of you that brings a peaceful power to my mind. Love is a way of looking at you that puts all you do in light. Your moods become ways of understanding you. Your faults become part of your charm. And yet my mind can also think of you carelessly and turn your affection into inconvenience, your friendship into a burden, and even see all you do as an attack. You can be my guide to pain or to rest. My mind can cradle you or crush you. The choice is mine. Love is no mystery, it is merely my decision to make of you a deeply considered and very comfortable subject.

I cannot offer you the flare of a newly lit fire. For although love warms, it does not burn at all. My body is familiar to you now. It cannot give you conquest. It has become a little frayed and is no triumph over those who once might have looked with envy at your having me. But it can offer you affection without anxiety and many small comforts. My arms can still hold you and my words support you. And every time I touch you you will know that nothing fleeting motivates me. You can take all the pleasures I give into your heart, and they will not hurt. Nor will they vanish like youth or grow ugly like lust. They will simply lighten your load and soften your path, and bring you a rest that knows no end.

Perhaps your birthday should remind me of how we
once were and of how much older we have become.
But it speaks softly to me of today. Today your
face is a more welcome sight, your touch more
affecting, from years of proven friendship. As a
great river deepens its bed, love has etched your
hands and face, and today you walk in true beauty.

The world makes so much of time—using it well, not having enough left, having wasted it, running out of it. During youth it seems there's never a sufficient amount for all that you long to do, then suddenly you are old and this great slowing down begins. Time stretches before you like a flat dead road that will never end, and you can't imagine how you will ever fill it. The opposite of time is now, but now has nothing to do with refusing to organize or plan or refer to the future, because now is not a behavior. It is the natural resting place of the heart, the one home where we feel at home. Now is a door that is forever open and will wait for us always. It is below us and above and all around, and only in our minds can we leave it.

All speech and bodily action pertain to the past and future. Either we are correcting what has happened or preparing for what might happen. Merely stopping at a grocery store is a form of planning. Unlike the body, however, the mind can dwell in the present because the present is peace, and from this peace it can correct and plan and make all necessary decisions. But when the mind forces the body to *appear* to "live in the now," it has itself leaned out of the present and become centered in a goal.

We can have either external consistency or internal consistency, either form or content. We cannot have both.

We look at the world, and at the events of our life in particular, thinking it has some lesson to teach us, and the only lesson we find is confusion. We believe some way can be found to interpret it, but confusion cannot be interpreted. The world tortures us only because we pour our hopes and yearnings over it, recalling and assessing every detail of its insanity, trying to make some sense of what just happened, trying to come up with a set of rules that will finally work, that will guide us safely through. But in a world of danger, how can we know refuge? In a world wrapped in darkness, how can we know light? The light is a circle that runs between all hearts and is found in the knowledge, born of kindness, that we are not alone. When we turn on each other and refuse to understand, we prove to our confusion that we *are* alone and cast ourselves back into night. The world is rutted and broken, and its story always ends the same. When we take each other's hand we can step more easily over its rubble and journey to a place so gentle in its reality that concern for the meaningless is undone, and we rest content simply to bless the world, and leave it unjudged and undisturbed.

Now has a thousand other names—commitment, awareness, concentration, rest, peace, love—but it is one experience, the only experience that truly matters. So sink into the welcoming arms of the present. Lie back on the breast of love, never to know worry again. There is no other place to go. There is nothing else to do. For I am with you, and we are one. Now and forever, and forever now.

There is no truth outside the mind's purity, outside
the riches of the soul. There is no truth in the insane
confusion of the world. Truth does not stand as some
monument to folly. And yet you reduce truth to merely
that whenever you think you have found a convenient
truth to *use*. To break truth into rules is to place
yourself outside of it.

Fall back into truth. Be consumed by your goodness.
You do not even know your own best interests. Truth
protects you because it is *greater* than you.

We have this overall view of our lives. We have this sense of its scope and direction, of "how we are doing," of "how things are going." And as we consult this impression we make attempts to get our life on course, or to give it meaning by changing our career, our partner, our residence, our body, our opinions. None of this has anything to do with love. Love can't be seen in the overall picture but in the moment-by-moment activities. How does one lie in bed on awakening? How does one go into the bathroom? How does one greet one's children? How does one get dressed?

It is not what we are doing but the peace with which we are doing it that contributes to the world.

Will the time come when we won't have to work so hard on our relationship? No, the time will come when there will be no lapse in our efforts. The time will come when it will be unthinkable for us to take a break from kindness.

All we will have left at the end of our lives is how we have treated each other and ourselves.

Love is the only I and the only Us. We do not lose but find ourselves in Love. There are no little I's, no isolated beings, no "entities," even though the mind can deceive itself into thinking it is alone. Yet one instant of kindness can restore the recognition that we live and dwell in each other.

You will know you are in love
when light shines
not only from the eyes of your beloved
but from the eyes of every face in the night

You will know you are in love
when your thoughts no longer peck inquiringly
at each other's minds
but soar like the wings of a single heart

Now the world below you
having nothing to fear from your laughter
rests
certain of your warm and knowing gaze

And because you are in love
you watch over it
watchful no more of each other

While we are apart . . .

we will simply hold hands across time
smile into each other's minds
and bask in the warmth of our love

To the reader:

This book has ended in a series of positive statements, but possibly it would have been more realistic to have closed with an entry about the arrival of a new problem. Any problem would do. The essential recognition is that two people do *not* finally arrive at a state in which concentration is no longer needed and can now fall back into their separate egos and rest. Separateness offers no rest, and the world never stops presenting sufficient reason to be miserable.

In a real relationship the couple have shifted their focus from the destination to the journey. Now their interest is in bringing kindness into each little activity and not in where the events of their relationship will finally take them. A real relationship cannot be pictured in advance. It does not of necessity include what is thought of as "good sex," or even any sex at all. It does not of necessity include having a child, owning a house, being in good health, or having financial security. It is the decision that I will love you and you will love me regardless of what this day brings.

Before this lesson is learned most couples direct their efforts toward manifesting an ideal that they absorbed early in life and that has been reinforced by songs written to sell, stories contrived to entertain, movies and TV dramas in which everyone is acting, and especially by the nonsense that friends and acquaintances feel obliged to feed each other about what they each deserve.

You will be happy in proportion to how continuously you attempt to understand your partner. Nothing short of this approach can bring you the deep, rich satisfaction you want and have a right to. Every day you are presented with a thousand opportunities to view some event, some thought, some mood as more pressing than being a friend. Every day your partner will seem to forget more often than you, and then the question will rise in your mind, Why should I try when this other person never does? As long as that seems a plausible point, you still doubt that it is happier to feel love than attack.

As has been stressed so often, feeling love has nothing to do with behavior, with mere form, with agreeing to demands or acting nice. It is a vision, a deeper reaction, a way of looking, an internal response. We *decide* to continue seeing our partner as our chosen friend, we *decide* to know why we are with this person, we *decide* that we are worthy of giving love.

The question "What have I got to show for it?" cannot accurately assess our happiness. For the most part, outcomes are not controllable and in fact often have remarkably little relationship to the process that led up to them. Our son John recently discovered this for himself. He is a natural hitter to begin with and in preparation for his Little League playoff game he worked even harder than usual, using both visualization techniques and increased batting practices. When the big moment came—bases loaded, two outs, and a hit needed to keep the rally going that could tie the game—he struck out. Likewise, the books that we have worked hardest on and are our best in terms of both content and quality of writing, are not always the best sellers. Nor are they always the worst. There is simply very little connection. As writers, then, for what should we live our lives? How should we judge our efforts? From what should we expect our reward? From the process of writing itself and not from what writing may or may not lead to.

In relationships, the same unpredictable and ungovernable nature of outcomes holds. Those who have the highest motives in choosing their mate do not, because of that, end up with, for example, someone who is financially successful or someone who will not die young. Those who work hardest on their relationship do not necessarily have fewer fights or stay together longer. The reality and happiness of the relationship lies in commitment to the process, not to the outcome; to trying, not to results; to daily attitude, not to expectations.

A happy couple are two who no longer wait. A happy couple are two who love for the sake of loving, who understand because it is freeing, who are kind because it sits better with the soul. They do not count on special treatment from life because of their efforts.

If we as a couple have made progress, you probably couldn't tell it by looking at us, our children, our animals, or our housekeeping. But if you could slip into our hearts and compare what you feel there with what was present twenty-five years ago, you would agree that our efforts have led to a result of a different kind. Things are different between us because they are more the same. We are happier today only because we have learned to choose happiness more often throughout the day. Yet when we forget, we experience the consequences of this mistake as emphatically as we did at the start of our marriage.

Our wish for those who read the thoughts we have recorded in this book, thoughts that for us have been like little lights that have danced before us and led us through a night that so often seemed impenetrable, is that you will never be afraid to believe in the possibility of love, of peace between two hearts, of lasting and unconditional devotion. There is a reality beyond the confusion of the world. It is experienced once you come to see that what blesses another blesses you. In that moment fear is lifted and hope is translated into certainty. And love is seen no longer as a possession, but as that which possesses you, and is you, and is all you ever need be.

Hugh and Gayle Prather
Spring 1989
Santa Cruz

ABOUT THE AUTHORS

In the year that Robert Audrey was pointing out that the mating range of a human was the same as a mosquito, Hugh and Gayle moved next door to each other in a small apartment building in Dallas. Despite their proximity, it was not until several months later that they first noticed each other. At two A.M., Gayle returned a box of Hugh's personalized checks that her boyfriend had stolen from the building's mail bin. Hugh's roommates did not believe her story and told him that she was making a pass. Consequently he soon invited her out, and on their third date, being unable to think of anything else to do, they crossed the state line and got married. Both knew they had made a mistake and set about to prove it.

The moral of their twenty-five-year marriage is that persistent effort toward the single goal of friendship can succeed despite conflicting values, personality differences, financial problems, sexual difficulties, and the sudden necessity of caring for a teenage boy from another marriage. Having no one to guide them, they had to learn all aspects of relating to each other by themselves. This they have done, and their life work has become helping other couples do the same.

As ministers they have married and counseled hundreds of couples; they have given numerous workshops on relationships, demonstrating especially their technique for "how to argue in peace"; and their last three books—*Notes on How to Live in the World . . . and Still Be Happy, A Book for Couples,* and *Notes to Each Other*—are specifically addressed to relationships and the exigencies of daily life.

Hugh Prather has been called "an American Kahlil Gibran" by *The New York Times,* and "one of the most compelling, insightful, inspirational, spiritual authors of our times" by *New Realities* magazine. Of his wife, Hugh writes, "Gayle is simply the kindest, most egoless, most intuitive entity on the planet."

The Prathers and their two boys, John and Jordan, live in the hills of Aptos, California, together with eight chickens, three goldfish, two rabbits, their cat, Tuba, and their dog, Kokomo Jones.